D1522938

my shalom
my peace

McGRAW-HILL BOOK COMPANY

NEW YORK   ST. LOUIS   SAN FRANCISCO   TORONTO

my shalom my peace

paintings and poems by jewish and arab children

MY SHALOM, MY PEACE

My Shalom, my Peace, is hidden in every broad smile.
In every cheerful look —
My Shalom, my Peace.
It smiles at me, this Shalom of mine,
From the laughing blue eyes of a child,
From children playing in the streets,
It winks at me, my Shalom, my Peace.
And it is always around, this Shalom of mine,
Like Hope which to the heart is bound,
This Peace of mine everywhere, always will be found.

Margit Cohn, Age 15, Ashdod

EDITED AND DESIGNED BY JACOB ZIM

SELECTION OF POEMS BY URIEL OFEK

TRANSLATION OF POEMS BY DOV VARDI

First published in Hebrew under the title **Hashalom Sheli** ©1974
by the American Israel Publishing Co. Ltd., and Sonol, Israel Ltd.
English translation copyright © 1975 by Sabra Books, Tel Aviv.
All rights reserved. No part of this publication may be reproduced,
stored in a retrieval system, or transmitted, in any form or by any means,
electronic, mechanical, photocopying, recording, or otherwise, without the
prior written permission of the publisher.

Library of Congress Cataloging in Publication Data
Main entry under title :
My shalom, my peace.
Translation of ha-Shalom sheli.
''The poem, My shalom, my peace, by Margit Cohn'': p. 3
SUMMARY : A collection of award-winning paintings,
and poems on the theme of peace, by Jewish
and Arab school children.
1. Children's writings, Israeli. 2. Israeli poetry — translations into English. 3. English
poetry — translations from Hebrew. 4. Peace — Poetry. [1. Israeli poetry — Collections.
2. Peace — Poetry] I. Zim, Jacob, ed. II. Ofek, Uriel, ed. III. Vardi, Dov, tr.
PJ5059. E3M9   892.4'1'60803   75-2493
ISBN   0-07-072826-7
Printed in Israel by Levanda Press.
Plates by Reshet Kav
Color separations by Plushnik Offset

PRAYER

What shall I ask You for, God?
I have everything.
There's nothing I lack.
I ask only for one thing
And not for myself alone;
It's for many mothers, and children, and fathers —
Not just in this land, but in many lands hostile to each other
I'd like to ask for Peace.
Yes, it's Peace I want,
And You, You won't deny the single wish of a girl.
You created the Land of Peace,
Where stands the City of Peace,
Where stood the Temple of Peace,
But where still there is no Peace...

What shall I ask You for, God? I have everything.
Peace is what I ask for,
Only Peace.

Shlomit Grossberg, Age 13, Jerusalem

DEDICATED IN PEAC

ND FRIENDSHIP TO THE CHILDREN OF THE WORLD

THE PAINT-BOX

I had a paint-box —
Each color glowing with delight;
I had a paint-box with colors
Warm and cool and bright.
I had no red for wounds and blood,
I had no black for an orphaned child,
I had no white for the face of the dead,
I had no yellow for burning sands.
I had orange for joy and life,
I had green for buds and blooms,
I had blue for clear bright skies.
I had pink for dreams and rest.
I sat down
and painted
Peace.

Tali Shurek, Age 13, Beer Sheva

I ASKED A SOLDIER

I asked a soldier in the street:
Peace, is it bitter or sweet?
Replied the soldier to my questioning:
Peace is a wonderful thing!
There are no bombs, no one shoots at you,
And you can live life quietly through.

I turned to my mother asking:
Peace, is it a positive or negative thing?
My mother replied:
Peace is joy and light!
We need Peace, Shalom,
So daddy will come home.

I asked my brother, the youngest one,
Back home from school, Grade One:
Tell me, what did you learn today?
He replied: We wrote "Shalom" and went to play,
To our enemy we shall give a hand
And live at peace in the Land.

Elad Tabachnik, Age 11, Ramatayim

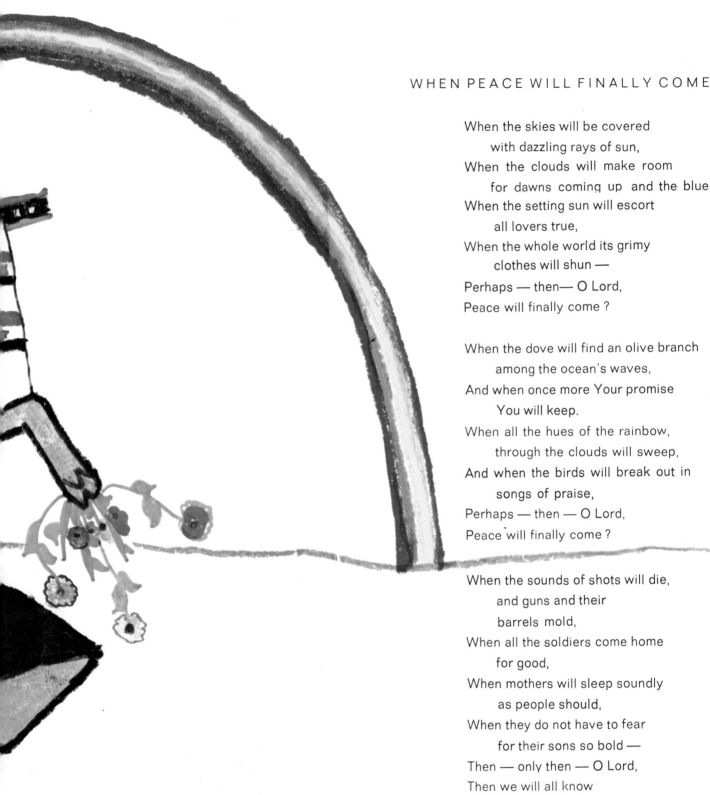

WHEN PEACE WILL FINALLY COME

When the skies will be covered
   with dazzling rays of sun,
When the clouds will make room
   for dawns coming up and the blue,
When the setting sun will escort
   all lovers true,
When the whole world its grimy
   clothes will shun —
Perhaps — then— O Lord,
Peace will finally come ?

When the dove will find an olive branch
   among the ocean's waves,
And when once more Your promise
   You will keep.
When all the hues of the rainbow,
   through the clouds will sweep,
And when the birds will break out in
   songs of praise,
Perhaps — then — O Lord,
Peace will finally come ?

When the sounds of shots will die,
   and guns and their
   barrels mold,
When all the soldiers come home
   for good,
When mothers will sleep soundly
   as people should,
When they do not have to fear
   for their sons so bold —
Then — only then — O Lord,
Then we will all know
That Peace is come...

Revital Ezrahi, Age 13½, Kiryat Motzkin

15

FREEDOM BIRD

Tell me, tell me, freedom bird
How will they stop the guns
    from shooting.
Bring us Peace, bring Shalom
Freedom bird, freedom bird
Bring us Peace,
Shalom.

Michal Sharon, Age 7, Savyon

צִפּוֹר דְּרוֹר, דַּבְּרִי, דַּבְּרִי
אֵיךְ יַפְסִיקוּ יְרִיּוֹת בָּעוֹלָם
פֶּן שְׁלַךְ שָׁלוֹם שָׁלוֹם
צִפּוֹר דְּרוֹר צִפּוֹר דְּרוֹר,
פֶּן שְׁלַךְ שָׁלוֹם,
שָׁלוֹם.

17

I AM PEACE

I am Peace
And Peace is me
A human being — that's me
Born for Peace
Disturb me not
You clanging metals
Of guns and armor plates
Of planes taking off to battle
Because Peace — that's me.

Baruh Ron, Age 8½, Ramat Gan

הَשׁלֹום זֶה אֲנִי
וַאֲנִי זֶה הַשָׁלֹום
בֶּן אָדָם אֲנִי
זֶה שָׁלֹום נֹולַדְתִּי
עַל תַּפְרִיעוּ
בְּרַעַשׁ מַתַּכֹות
תֹותָחִים שִׁרְיֹונֹות
וּמְטֹוסִים עַל הַקְּרָב
כִּי שָׁלֹום זֶה אֲנִי.

THE CRY FOR PEACE

The words described a battle
 of armored forces clashing,
The lines of print told of planes engaged,
The pen whispered about the brave,
The paper absorbed the thunder of shells...
But this is not what I want to write about.
I want to write
About the cry for Peace
Bursting from the bazooka's jaw
At the foot of the uniformed figure;
About the prayer for Peace
You see in the eyes of officers
       in the War Room.
About the call for Peace
Cleaving air,
Bombshells are splitting.
About the prayer for Peace
From the mouths of those calling out:
       "After me !"
From the mouths of the fallen,
From the mouths of the wounded,
From the mouths of civilians,
       soldiers and children —
Peace!

Frida Zeitelbah, Age 14, Haifa

TO DREAM OF PEACE

Peace is like dreaming
    of something eternal,
A fairy tale both old and new;
With its heroes — the good and the evil,
The love of life and of death, too.
To dream of Peace is like thinking of a world
With sorrow, anger and hate.
There's a marvelous ending
    to this story of blood,
Although it's far away beyond the gate...

To dream of Peace in the evening glow
And in the morning, early to rise,
To dream of Peace and suddenly to know
That such it will be, not otherwise.

Nitsa Sha'shua, Age 13, Tel Aviv

24

25

OFF TO THE ARMY

Off to the army, my Daddy went
To guard the borders he was sent
And from the Negev and up to Golan.
The enemy just saw him and ran,
And when he came home a long time after
I thought they had shut the army down
That peace had come for good.
But again Daddy got the call
And then I understood
That peace hadn't come at all.

Eliav Brand, Age 6½, Tel Aviv

WHAT I SHOULD LIKE TO DO

We'll pick narcissus along the trail;
Down avenues of palm we'll make our way;
In the blue Kinnereth we'll dip and sail;
When Peace will come, some day,

My dad in uniform, then to embrace,
And visits to my brother, Eyal, at his base,
This is what I should like to do:
If Peace would only come for true.

To send a card with the word,
Greetings to every state in the world,
To bless them in this people's name
For Peace which finally came.

Matti Yosef, Age 9, Bat Yam

WE WILL GET YOU

Peace, we will get you,
Wherever you may be.
Even though still a dream
Today,
We will get you, Peace.

With flowers will we deck
The gun barrels,
And the young soldiers'
Heads
Cover with wreaths.

Even you be delayed,
We shall not lose hope.
We shall keep our fingers warm
For you
And there will be no more wars.

We shall overcome every enemy with songs of Peace
And the world will be quiet.
Please, then,
Do not run away,
Wait,
And let there be no more wars.

Shalom Rufeisen, Age 14, Kibbutz Reshafim

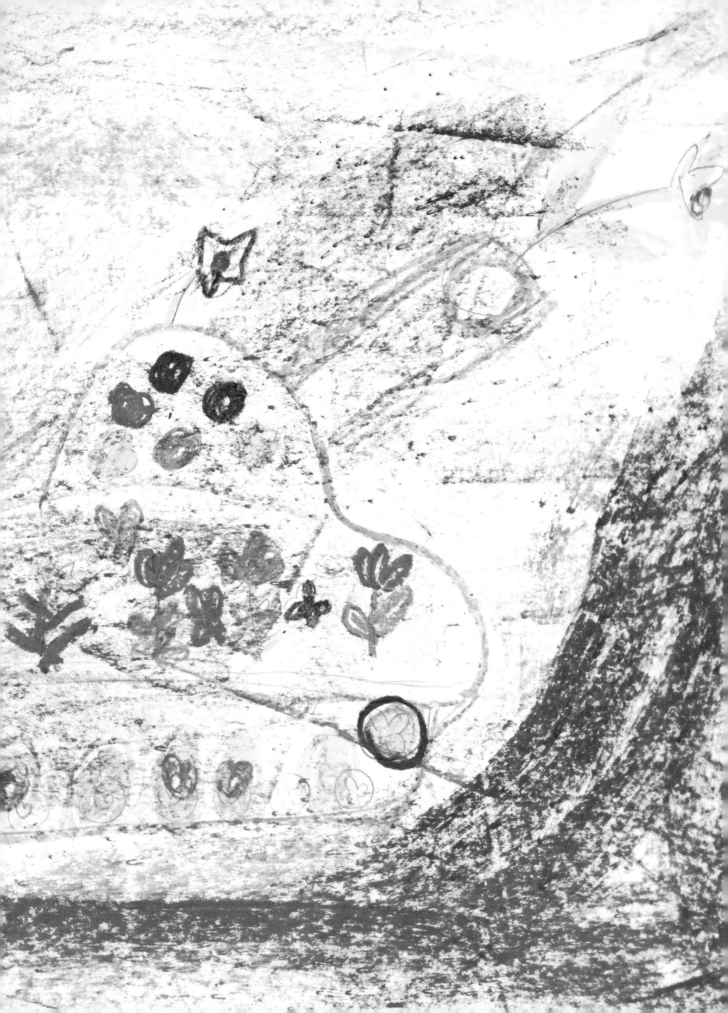

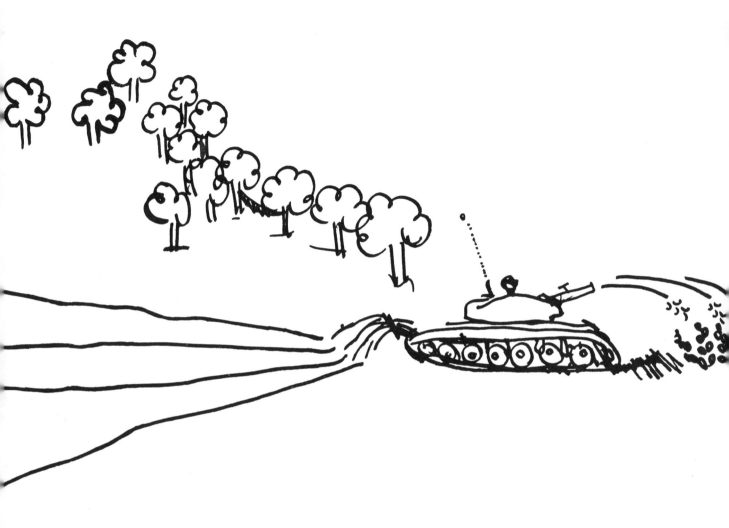

THE LITTLE PIPER

"Look, girl," said my soldier friend, a fellow nice and young:
"Peace won't just come dropping in one day.
But it's good to wait for it — even more to hope, I must say.
It's much better than sitting around weeping over battles and wars.
Yes, Peace won't be a big surprise, but a day will come
When we'll be able to say for certain: it is here!
The day on which all the fronts will be calm,
        and the borders still, my dear,
While over them women will be peacefully hanging out
        their laundry.
People won't kill each other and man won't rise against man,
There'll be no more lands destroyed, or blood pouring away."

My friend stopped talking then just saying, "Go in Peace!"
And last night, returning home, I dreamed a dream I love,
I dreamed of skies completely blue, and not a cloud above.
Below, a sea becalmed and little children laughing,
When lo, from somewhere off the horizon, far, far away
We could make out a little child quietly walking ahead,
A pipe in his mouth, his clothes worn to a thread,
And following his tune, armaments moving in array,
Charmed by his music, all the instruments of war and
        destruction,
Departing from the world forever, with him and his pipe leading
        the way.

Rona Shahar, Age 12½, Tel Aviv

A COLORED DREAM

I dreamed a dream yesterday,
And it was colored, too,
Many colors of different hue,
Red and grey,
The brightest brown you've ever seen,
And around the edges, a touch of green.

I dreamed of war and the blood of men
Running among the grey stones then;
Of tanks with the brightest brown you've ever seen
And khaki uniforms with touches of green.
I thought an Egyptian was coming near...
And suddenly I woke from my dream in fear.

Tonight I dreamed a dream
In many colors again;
Violet and green,
White and blue
And the brightest brown
Almost flooding the whole town.
Green lawns and purple blooms,
The sun shining in a sky all blue;
With a cooing dove the heavens gracing,
And below, a child, her father embracing.

Put briefly — Peace is good
If it would only come soon — it should!

Lea Miller, Age 9, Haifa

Когда уже придёт мир?

Мы долго мечтали о мире
Воюя в неравных боях
Хоронили в братских могилах
Грезя о светлых днях
И даже в дни побед и перемирий
Спокойно спать мы не могли
И просыпались от сновидений
В кошмарном ужасе войны
Сколько сынов в боях мы потеряли
Сколько рек крови унесла война
Солдаты погибая знали
Что Родина у них одна
И каждого ждал кто-то дома
Платая слёза и просмотрев глаза
Но мысль о мире нас не покидала
Когда уж кончится война?
Когда придёт уж время мира
Мы ждём его не день, не год, а четверть
века
Когда наступит тишина?
И кончится война!!!

Сочинили этот стих
Ганни Шор и Шимон Тепер
(Имми хадашим из СССР)
Авторам стиха - 14 лет.
Школа: "Уафричили"
Город: Хадера

FOR LONG WE DREAMED

For long we dreamed of Peace
     and all its good,
As we, a few, against the enemy fought.
We, at our brothers' graves
     in silence stood
And of better days, dreamed
     and thought.
And even during a cease-fire
     or victories,
We could not sleep for fear
     and dread,
Because we dreamed of horrors
     and calamities

And saw only wars and their dead.
So much blood flowing in rivers.
So many sons lost to their mothers,
But the men knew with their
     dying shivers :
One is the Land of our Fathers,
     none other.
And back home, each one
     was being expected.
A look of despair,
     from the eyes — a tear,
But the hope for Peace
     has not been rejected.
O, when will wars at last end here?
When will Peace come to us too?
We've been waiting for it

     not a day or a month, but 25 years.
When will there be quiet,
     and dreams come true,
An end to wars, to shooting
     and fears ?...

Hayim Shor and Shimon Tepper, Age 14, Hadera
    (New immigrants from Russia)

AT LAST

Now all fighting has ceased;
He who made man, has brought Peace.
People are glad and babies are happy.
Little boys and girls, hands are clapping.
There's such a pleasant air,
No more fighting anywhere.
Old folks and children are playing together,
No one is running down to the shelter.
It's calm and quiet, everyone satisfied —
Peace at last in this great world and wide!

Anat Hatzor, Age 7, Givat Brenner

GENEALOGICAL TREE

Translation of Arabic calligraphy — two lines at top : "We are
   two branches of the same thick and leafy tree.
We are and will remain as we were, if only we reach
   an understanding."
The lower part of the trunk: "Abraham."
The branch on the right: "Ishmael"; on the left: "Isaac."
On the tree-top on the right: "the Arabs"; on the left: "the Jews."

40

THE TUNNEL OF PEACE

Should I come across
      the tunnel of Peace —
I shall go down and cut out
      its most precious delicacy,
And spread it among human beings everywhere,
      for Peace to rule over land and sea.
Nations inimical, then, the sons of the same race,
Who were always meeting only in battle,
      now will mutually embrace,
And conciliated, at last each other bless,
Looking up and weeping with joy
      as one another they address.
Then will they go to the sacred river,
      the river of Peace,
Their weapons break there
      and their guns to the deep release,
They will melt down their planes
      and into ploughshares beat their swords.
To fulfill the worthy Isaiah's admirable words.
Then will our lives be relieved
      of disappointment and despair,
Our afflictions and grief disappear;
From every spot and habitation, all hatreds gone,
Buried our fears, with a past we shall not mourn.

Come then, come to the Tree-of-Peace,
Let us shake each other's hands
      extended in Peace,
So that we may live lives of joy
      and happiness to come —
Come then, come together, come!

Ghassan Sarsour, Age 13½, Kfar Kassem (Arab village)

حلم السلام
حين اعش على نجم السلام

ارحله واقتلع معدن السلام النفيس

اوزعه على الناس سبيل السلام

ديلتقي الناس من مختلف الشعوب

فو ساحات المعارك والقتال

يتعانقون ، يتصالحون ويكون كذا الفرح

فتنساب دموعهم لتلتقي في النهر المقدس

في "نهر السلام"

يحطمون الاسلحه والطائرات والمدافع

يصهرونها ويحولون السيوف إلى مناجل

لتتحقق نبوءة أشعيا

وينزول التشاؤم من حياتنا

لتمحق آلامنا واحزاننا ويمحق العداء من الوجود

فتنجلي همومنا وننعم بالحياة

ونندفن ما ض لن يعود

الاسم الكامل : غسان عبد الرحمن يوسف سرسور
كفر قاسم ، المثلثه ، بريد بيتح تكفا
العمر : ١٣.٥ سنه
مدرسة كفر قاسم "ب"
الصف الثامن

YOU DIDN'T COME

We built you a city and a tower,
A street we dedicated
    in your name;
Doves we prepared,
    trees and flowers
Woods and fields
But you — you didn't come!

Poems we composed,
    prayers, songs of praise
A story we wrote, a photo
    we took
And made a painting too —
But you — you didn't come!

We even made sacrifice
Life itself we gave
But you — you didn't come!

So tell me, tell me
What is it we haven't given you
    and we shall prepare it,
Shall offer and present it
Just say what,
    but come to us already —
Peace!

Nava Caspi, Age 15½, Jerusalem

THE HOVERING DOVE

When the echoes of bursting shells will die,
When once again Peace will reign
    in every home and field —
White and pure, a dove will hover in the sky
And in its beak, an olive branch like a shield.

A hovering dove, its color pure and white
Above each home and garden, watch it now;
Anxious workers in the field follow its flight
And the eagle too, its head to her will bow.

Toward the borders, flying then a dove,
Upward, every farmer lifting his face;
Light clouds floating by above,
The sun warming it with golden rays.
And when to both sides of the border
    night brings cover.
Bearing in its fold a dream,
A hollow tree trunk the dove will discover,
Sleeping there till day will beam.

And when beyond the mountains
    the sun will rise,
And the remnants of the dream erase,
Among a thousand birds, the dove now flies,
While behind it the Messiah of Peace
    follows apace.

Miky Maltc, Age 10, Kiryat Motzkin

I DON'T LIKE WARS

I don't like wars
They end up with monuments;
I don't want battles to roar
Even in neighboring continents.

I like Spring
Flowers producing,
Fields covered with green,
The wind in the hills whistling.

Drops of dew I love,
The scent of jasmine as night cools,
Stars in darkness above.
And rain singing in pools.

I don't like wars. They end
In wreaths and monuments;
I like Peace come to stay
And it will some day.

Matti Yosef, Age 9, Bat Yam

FATHER AND SON

He has always wept and suffered without end,
He wanted just this once
To live again with his Dad
Through those pleasant childhood days
When they would walk together hand in hand,
When a warm hand used to take him to school
And he not wanting to part.
Then came the war, and the hand was cut off
Forever and ever.

The Arab boy also feels suffering.
He wanted just this once, again he wanted —
To pass with his father through the same village.
The chickens clucking, the cattle lowing
And the two of them happy and singing
      a lively tune...
But the war silenced the song,
A love song of a father and his son...

O why the immense hate?
Why shouldn't there be
Peace?

Amit Tal, Age 11, Haifa

PEACE IS GOOD

When Peace will come, come indeed,
When the dream will finally be true,
When Messiah will come riding
        on his great white steed,
Solid gold through and through,
And in his hand a banner hold
To show that our expectations
        have taken place —
Then husband and son, and father old
Need no more danger face
And a little girl will not ask
        her mother anymore,
"But Mommy, who needs war?"
Then in the shops they'll sell
Building blocks and every sort of animal,
While in town and village, little boys
Will no more know of guns for toys,
 And person to person will smile
        instead
For Peace is good: I bet you lots!
No more wounded, no more dead,
No more shelters, no more shots;
And where once there was only
        the bitter sigh,
You will hear singing with spirits high.

Tami Ha'Elyon, Age 9½, Tel Aviv

MUHAMMED AND ME

When Peace will come to be,
Down the pathways we will run,
Among the grass in the orchard.
Muhammed and me.

When Peace will come,
I'll give my hand to Muhammed,
To the Jordan we will go.
Together sing and hum.

When Peace will be on every side,
Arm in arm shall we go
The two of us hiking all over —
And up to Jerusalem, we'll take a ride.

When Peace will come and fighting ends,
We shall walk then, holding hands,
As far as Gilead —
Two happy friends.

Tamar Sharon, Age 9½, Savyon

A PITY

A pity, a pity, all this has been
So let's forget and start again.
Go on, go on and never cease
To love tomorrow's Peace.

Give us strength to forget
The terrible nightmare of war
The strength to smile and happy be,
To live on in our home, our State,
        and free;

Live on through Yom Kippur days.
Hear the Shofar blow and not
        the sirens scream,
Year after year remember those
        who fell in the strife —
It is they who entrusted us with life.

Idan Brayer, Age 10, Ashkelon

BLESSED ART THOU

Blessed art Thou, Blessed Lord,
Bring Peace to this Land, an end to the sword!
Let's turn each helmet into a flower pot
And all the shining brass throw out to rot.

We'll take our holidays in the Lebanon
And the Egyptians, theirs, on Mount Hermon;
Over the border, schools we'll build
For Jews and Arabs, where once men were killed.

Swings we'll hang from the barrels of guns,
Across revolvers, spiders will spin their runs;
Daddy will sit around and read his paper at ease,
Instead of going up north to fight and freeze.

The battle-field is now used for play
Where thousands of children come every day;
Finally they'll stop the spilling of blood,
Peace will come and battles be over for good.

And when Daddy from the war returns, then
He'll never don his uniform again;
And on Purim I won't dress up like a soldier as before.
Because such things simply won't be anymore.

Efrat Shiler, Age 11, Holon

PEACE IS

Peace is a moon looking down over the city,
With the city white and still and calm,
Peace is sounds of joy striking your ears
And the city laughing with tears.

Peace is like an old grandpa
        spreading his cloak in the skies
And sailing children across a world
        with no borders on land or water,
His beard is long, hoary and white,
While blue are his eyes, the color of the sea, quite.

Peace is the song of the farmers at harvest
Going out to the fields with a smile on their lips;
Children singing, laughter and dancing,
Bright stars and skies entrancing.

Sparrows on the tree-tops twitter,
In the field, the rustling grain:
"Peace, Peace, such a wonderful thing,"
The wind among the corn is whispering.

And when Peace comes to field and garden
And all the rifles disappear —
The entire land will dress in holiday best
And the sun shine seventy-fold till it goes to rest.

Michele Chozon, Age 13, Tel Aviv

WE'LL KNOW

When doubly it will shine, the sun,
When the skies will be blue
      times seventy,
When the loveliest of flowers
      will bloom in plenty —
We'll know that Peace has come.

When children on the border,
      to shelters will not run,
When no more we will hear the guns
      that roar,
When in peace and quiet we will sleep
      as we did before,
We'll know that Peace has come.

When we'll be able to ride all over
      Egypt and Lebanon,
On the Hermon, not be afraid of skiing,
Through Syria, be able to go hiking —
We'll know that Peace has come.

When we'll hear no more of killed and wounded,
When we'll no more fear terrorists who raid.
When border villages will no more be afraid,
We'll know that Peace has come.

When swords will be beaten into ploughshares,
When kindergartens and schools the
        watchmen no more will patrol,
When at eighteen, the army's not the goal,
Then we'll know, Peace has come.

Ayelet Epstein, Age 13½, Even Yehuda

O, MOTHER MINE

In my dream, O mother mine,
I saw an angel with wings pure white
Breaking the rifles one by one,
Shattering to pieces each gun,
Which then into the fire he dashes
And turns into smouldering ashes.

In my dream, O mother mine,
I saw an angel with wings pure white
Scattering the ashes clean
Over the glittering scene.
And the ashes turning into a white dove,
Hovering over the East, jubilant above.

In my dream, O mother mine,
I saw an angel with wings pure white
Lifting Moses and Mohammed
        up to the skies
And demanding they shake hands
        and be wise.
I heard his voice thunder and echo
        after them:
Quick, make haste, O sons of Shem —
Behold he is coming, the herald of Peace,
Singing a song of praise to Peace.

Gassoub Serhan, Age 14, Kfar Yafia (Arab Village)

في الحلم يا أماه !
رأيت ملاكا ابيضا
يحطم البنادق
يفجر المدافع
يرقرق كلّ
فتصير رمادا

في الحلم يا أماه !
رأيت الملاك
ينثر الرماد
فيتحول الى حمام بيضاء
في قبة السماء ، فوق شرقنا لجبين

في الحلم يا أماه
رأيته يسلك يهود وموسى
فينزعهما على التصالح في العناق

في الحلم يا أماه !
صيحته ينثر
يعتز يقول
هبا يا ابناء سام
ننشر أحلى انا استير السلام
فغدا سياتي رسول السلام !

69

PEACE IS WORTH MORE

When, O when, will the dream come true,
That Israel be at Peace for me and you?
We are weary of grief, to bear it all,
The pain and losses, sorrow continual.
Peace is worth a thousand times more
Than all the guns and shells that roar.
When Peace will come, gardens will bloom
        without measure,
Because everybody will tend them with pleasure;
And then, when all quarrels come to an end,
We'll cross the Suez, our holidays to spend.
We'll ride to Egypt, Jordan and Lebanon,
No more guns, the defenders all gone;
We'll be able to visit and get to know
The Cedars of Lebanon, Petra and Cairo.
O, would there no more hatred be
And all the people, each other love to see.
Surely then, Peace — upon the world descend,
O, how much all of us upon you depend!

Tali Gat, Age 10, Holon

تحيه طيبه وبعد،،

ودد ان اكتب قصيدة في السلام مشاركه مني لمحبي السلام وارجو لنا يعم السلام في ارضنا

العمر:- ١٤ سنه

وهذه قصيدتي:-

السلام كلمة حق تجري على كل لسان

تقال في كل زمان ومكان

لتبرهن ان الانسان يحيى في امان

وليبعد عنا الحزن من شئ يسمى السلاح

ويعيد للكون كله الابتهاج

ويحميه من الدموع والجراح

ويرجع لنا بهجتنا

وينور لنا ان سكنتنا

يا ايها العالم انشدوا وغنيات السلام

لنعيش في حياة لمحبة الدوام

لنمشي السنين كلها في احلام

لا نعرف اير يبقى الحزن ولاولد الظلام

نتمنى للسلام ولمحبى وسلام

The writer, Haled Aaref abu Sherifa, age 14, from the Arab village of Tul Karem, introduces his poem with the following words:
"My best wishes for Peace! I want to write a poem about Peace as my participation in the wishes for Peace, and the hope that it will come to our country."

A WORD OF TRUTH

Shalom is a word of truth common to every tongue,
Pronounced everywhere and every time,
To express the desire of the fathers to be tranquil and secure
To remove from us the suffering caused by so-called "arms."
To restore to the universe the canopy of joy
To protect it from tears and affliction.
O, you inhabitants of the world! Sing us the songs of Peace
For a life of love and friendship everlasting
So that the years of our life transpire like a pleasant dream
And of fear and care we know no more.

THE PEACE BALLOON

When Peace comes
I shall only ask for a little gift — a balloon.
But not just any balloon,
A special one,
A balloon tied to a kite across which
    is written the word
"Shalom!"

All over the world will I send the balloon.
And when the day comes, I shall look up above,
And this time the kite will return
Without a balloon but with a million Jews.
And then, when Peace comes to the world,
I will be happier than any person alive.

Rachel Sambursky, Age 7, Tel Aviv

WHEN MOTHER WAS ABOUT MY AGE

When mother was about my age
The War of Liberation had just begun,
And mother knew what Refugee Ships were
As well as a Sten, bullets and a gun.

When mother was about my age
"This is the final battle," was chanted night and day;
We have gone through three more wars since then,
And from Galilee and the Sharon, the border is now further away

Since then we have moved twenty-six years ahead,
We sing no more of the "final battle," but of the
     "final war" instead;
We know what a Mirage is like and a Phantom, too,
But it is time Peace should come into view.

Rakefet Sarig, Age 10½, Herzliya

76

أمنية. السلام

يا يا راية السلام
يا يا اجنحه الحمام
متى تغطين المعمورة
وتنحط ميل احلى اسطورة

FLAGS OF PEACE

O, flags of Peace, on every house they fly!
O, wings of the dove with olive branches in the sky!
When will you spread your blessings everywhere to view —
That the most beautiful tale of all's come true.

Fathey Mohamd Agbaria, Age 13½, Um Elfahm (Arab Village)

WHEN WILL IT COME, THE DAY

When will peace take over?
When will it come, the day?
When with armies and bombs will they do away
When all this hostility cease,
A day on which battleships
Will become palaces of leisure and fun
Floating on the seas.

A day on which the steel of guns
Will be melted into pleasure cars;
A day on which generals will begin to raise flowers.

When peace
Will include all the peoples of these neighboring lands,
When Ishmael and Israel
Will go hand in hand,
And when every Jew —
The Arab's brother will be.
When will it come, the day?

Mahmud Abu Radj, Age 12, Kfar Sachnin (Arab Village)

Dale una chance a la paz
varias veces con sus amigos, grité.
Era su Julio más lindo

Inexorables, pasaron los días
Estalló el conflicto y su ejército lo llamó.
Nuevamente grité

Esta vez, grité y amó
Fue en el campo de batalla.
Era su último octubre.

No Fue el primero que gritó por la paz
tampoco el único que luchando, cayó
fue uno más a quien la paz Frustró

Sé que seguiremos gritando
Sé que no cesaremos de luchar
Pero... paz, espéranos!

GIVE PEACE A CHANCE

Give Peace a chance
To his friends he would often cry out.
It was the most beautiful July in his life.

Pitiless were the days that followed,
Hostilities broke out
    and to the army he was called.
Again he cried out.
This time he cried out and loved as well.
It was on the battle-field.
The last October of his life.

He was not the first to cry out to Peace,
Not the only one who in battle fell.
He was just another one
    whom Peace deceived.

I know we will continue to cry out.
I know the battles will not end.
But . . . do wait for us, Peace !

Amnon Zeidenberg, Age 16, Bat Yam
    (new immigrant from South America)

PEACE IS A YOUNG MOTHER

Peace is a young mother
Walking with her son
Hand in hand,
A smile of happiness
On her face;
And you knowing
You will not have
To meet her again in the street
Ten years later
Wearing black,
Tearful and wrinkled
A look of endless grief
In her eyes
Which nothing can console.

Peace is all this
For us and for other people as well.
All this and much,
Much more.

Shai Ben Moshe, Age 13, Kfar Mordecai

SING THE SONGS OF PEACE

Peace — is a quiet land
Peace — is a flowering strand
Peace — is a happy mother
Peace — is a land without borders
Peace — is a boy who's not a soldier
Peace — isn't just a dream.

So sing, sing the songs of peace
And it'll come to us and never cease
No longer just a dream.

Peace — is a safe and quiet land
Peace — is a land without guards
Peace — is a country without siren alerts
Peace — is a five letter word
Peace — is a period of truth
Peace — isn't just a dream.

So sing, sing the songs of peace
And it'll come to us and never cease
No longer just a dream.

Doron Zazon, Age 9, Givat Nesher

A Bit of Peace

A bit of peace is needed
to make the bad wars stop.
The world will then be happy,
from the bottom to the top.

Many brave men get killed
in war after war after war.
A bit of peace is needed,
and wars will be no more.

If peace and war will ever meet
the peace will always win,
for peace is like a blessing
and war is like a sin.

Moshe Cohen, 11, Nahalal

COME SHALOM

To Gilboa, Tabor Mount
From above looks down
And news you wouldn't believe,
Sends with glee;
The Jordan into Kinnereth runs
And brings another rumor,
Long expected and familiar,
And yet, almost forgotten:
Come, come, come Peace,
Come, Shalom our Peace.

In the water the fish
Not with voices, but with eyes
One, two, three, transmit
The message of congratulations;
In the meadows, narcissus too,
The winds told them a secret
Hoping they wouldn't forget
To tell both me and you:
Come, come, come Peace,
Come, Shalom our Peace.

Nurith Peretz, Age 14½, Bat Yam

TOMORROW

When tomorrow I open my eyes
I should like to hear the news
All the children in the world
Are waiting for :
That Peace, the Redeemer has come.

Tomorrow,
No more yesterdays cruel,
When Daddies didn't come back from the wars.
Because tomorrow when Peace comes
The sun will shine in the skies
Everything will be blooming all about.
There'll be no guard-duty then,
And I'll travel to Egypt to make a friend.

Tomorrow, tomorrow on Peace Day
There'll be no orphans any more,
Not scared of terrorists, friends will come up north to visit
And we'll joke about times in the past
When we ran to shelters
And lessons missed...
Tomorrow, when peace comes, we won't waste money on arms
We'll buy more cows for our farms.

Vardit Fertouk, Age 8, Kibbutz Hagoshrim

THIS IS THE DAY

This is the day on which
    terror will turn into peace
And the ruins of battles
    to joy and creation;
The day on which hate
    into love will turn
And resentment
    into conciliation.

Then no more the heart
    will dread
That suddenly bereavement
    will strike;
Jews and Arabs together
    in the field,
Crops will produce alike.

Journey routes will go through
    Cairo, too
And borders won't be guarded
    in any way;
On a Saturday picnic, to Beirut
    we'll go,
Or in Damascus spend a day.

And the land will be still, the sun
    glowing red,
With brotherhood, friendship
    and delight, we'll be thrilled;
All nations Peace will splendidly
    observe
And people's hearts with love will
    be filled.

Michal Israeli, Age 12, Ma'ayan Zvi

SIGNS

If of seas and hills we continue to sing,
If somehow we think of all kinds of things,
If there still be some who with many colors paint,
Then perhaps together these are signs and more:
A sign that overhead the sun will still rise,
A sign that lilies will bloom white as before,
A sign that again the fields will be only green
And the skies not covered with clouds of red.

If yesterday we closed the shelters up,
And if cars as before honk their horns without stop,
If these be not tears but the wetness of rain,
And the street-lamps glowing once again —
It is a sign we may yet find the golden mean,
A sign that from now and forever we will only love,
A sign that one night a full moon will shine above —
And the Peace we have been seeking
        will be back on the scene.

Havatselet Levi, Age 14½, Rishon Le Zion

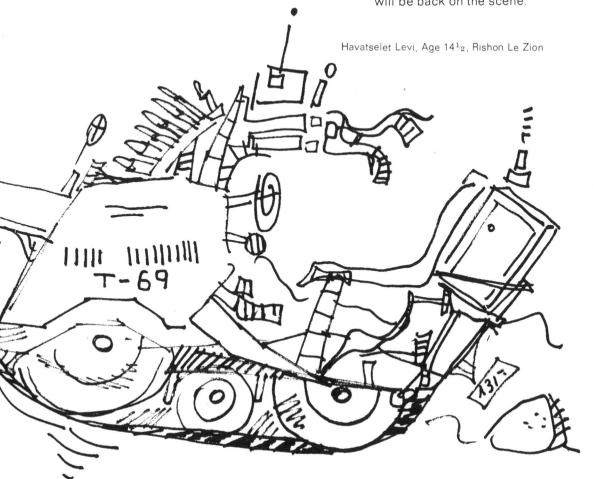

The illustrations in this book are by :